Make Mon...

50 Items That You C...

Ma...

Other Books by the Author:

Sell On EBay And Win: How to Start an eBay Empire with $100 By Marc Pierce

Make Money Online: 70 Painless Way to Make Money for $5 or Less By Marc Pierce

INTRODUCTION:

If you didn't know already, eBay is a goldmine when it comes to making money online. Yet, many people that try to sell items on there fail. It isn't because they didn't try hard or don't have the skills to succeed, it is simply because they aren't selling the right items.

I have read other eBay books and quite frankly, I was appalled at what I saw. The information only included eBay rules and its history, which isn't hard to figure out. The strategies in the books for finding quality items were to drive from department store to department store looking for discounted items. Well, if you plan on being successful selling on eBay that just won't cut it. How do I know? Because I make enough money on eBay alone to fully support myself and I know what works and what doesn't.

With all the blogs and books out there online, it is hard to find genuine information on how to make real money on eBay! However, I will change that for you today. This book is designed to tell you exactly what items sell on the platform, how you can find them, and how to sell them.

Years ago when I first started my entrepreneurial journey, I was broke and was making minimal income from my first business. I decided to try out eBay to bring in a much-needed income. After just a few months, I was making thousands of dollars every month. My method was simple, I found what sold, obtained it and I sold it.

With this book, you won't have to go through the ups and downs that I did. I will be your guide and tell you exactly what to buy, how to buy it, and inform you of the results you will get. Let me be your guide to help you start an eBay business or expand on the one you have.

#1 DESIGNER WOMEN'S HANDBAGS

Handbags have been one my best selling items throughout my reselling career. They are always in high demand and I never hold on to them long. The customer base for designer handbags seems to be endless and it is only getting bigger as time goes on. The Handbags that you sell must be in good to excellent shape and include detailed descriptions with multiple clear pictures. It is imperative that you only sell designer handbags. Non-brand name handbags will not sell and will cause you to hold on to them longer than you would like, but no worries there a enough designer bags to go around.

If you are selling the following brands you can't go wrong: B. Makowsky, Brighton, Burberry, Cartier, Chico's, Christian Dior, Coach, Cole Haan, Dolce & Gabbana, Dooney & Bourke, Fendi, Giorgio Armani, Gucci, Hermes, Juicy Couture ,Louis Vuitton, Marc Jacobs, Michael Kors, Neiman Marcus and Thirty-One.

#2 AUTHENTIC SPORTS JERSEYS

Authentic stitched professional sports jerseys (NFL, NBA or NHL) are extremely popular. In many cases the team and player isn't that significant, fans will find the team they love and will make a purchase. Diehard fans are common and love to show devotion to their team, which makes it easy for eBay sellers.

Along with current jerseys, Authentic Vintage jerseys are a hot buy. If you are able to come across a jersey that has been actually worn by the player, you will increase the price and if the player has signed the jersey the price will go up even further.

Best Player Jerseys to sell: Michael Jordan, Kobe Bryant, LeBron James, Magic Johnson

#3 COWBOY BOOTS

I still remember buying my first lot of Cowboy boots. I was so worried that I wouldn't be able to sell them. Surprisingly enough, it only took me a week to sell ten pairs of boats at very profitable margins. Cowboy boots come in a wide variety of styles and materials. Knowing what to look for will help you tremendously when selling them. Cowboy boots made out Alligator, Crocodile, leather, elephant hide, Ostrich and snakeskin are all amazing sellers. With the proper brand and material cowboy boots can sell up to $1,000, you can't go wrong with a high quality boot. You can buy boots to resell on clearance racks at popular shoe stores such as Designer Shoe Warehouse or though eBay lots by searching "cowboy boot lot" in the search field.

Brands that sell well: Lucchese, Tony Lama, Golden Goose, Liberty Boot Co, J. Chisholm, Nocona, Tony Lama, Laredo, Justin Boots, Durango, Dan Post

#4 HUNTING KNIVES

Hunting knives are one of those items that will sell in all parts of the country (USA). However, many customers will be in traditional hunting states such as Texas, Louisiana and Florida. Not only a great sell brand new; used, vintage and custom hunting knives can sell in the thousands.

Hunting knife Brands that sell well: Randall, Benchmade, Case, Gerber, Kershaw, Schrade

#5 MOTORCYCLES

Yes, you can sell various types of motorcycles on eBay and for a great return. This wildly popular item can fetch up $50,000 just for one high-end model. However, the typical price range for running vehicles is between $1,500 and $35,000. Not bad huh, Non-running motorcycles can sell for at least $500. If you are looking to make real money on eBay, motorcycles are the way to go.

Bestselling Motorcycle brands: Vintage Indian, Harley Davidson (All Models), New Model Slingshots, New Model Can-Ams, Honda Gold Wings, BMW R or K series and Yamaha YZF-R's.

#6 Travel Trailers

Do you have a travel trailer that you don't use or thinking of flipping a large ticket item? Well, you might be in luck. When I sold my first travel trailer, I was shocked at the money I made. The beauty of this item is that it sells brand new, broken or for its parts. In fact, did you know you can sell parts such as recliners, ovens and windows between $50 - $600? You can purchase a trailer from sites such as craigslist.org and resell it on eBay. The most you will receive for a single trailer will be close to $40,000. Average prices for travel trailers on eBay sell between $9,000- $11000, pretty good for a day's work I'd say.

Bestselling Travel Trailers brands: Airstream, New Lite Travel Trailers, Jayco, Keystone

#7 RVS

RV's will always sell on eBay and can make you amazing profits. Recreation Vehicles have been used by families for vacations, camping trips and cross country driving for years and this American traditional vehicle doesn't appear to be slowing down in sales anytime soon. RV's are very similar to travel trailers in the manner that they are sold except RV's are even more lucrative. You can sell RV's for up to $70,000 on the site. You can purchase RV's for resale on different sites such as cartrucktrader.com, Rvtrader.com, craigslist.org, rvs.oodle.com and cheap-rv-rental.com

Bestselling RVS: Fleetwood, Winnebago, Itasca and Georgie Boy

#8 BOATS

An enormous amount of boats are sold on eBay on a daily basis. The most lucrative type of boatS on the market are yachts and cabin cruisers. On any given day, boats can be sell for up to $150,000. However, there have been million dollar yachts that have sold on eBay. If you don't have a boat to sell currently, don't be discouraged. Boat parts such as outboard motors, propellers, fuel tanks and GPS's can sell for thousands of dollars. If you are looking to sell an item for a sizable profit boats are a great item to sell. Most Boats are sold via local pick up on eBay. Sites such as boattrader.com , yachtworld.com, craigslist.org and boats.iboats.com are great places to purchase boats for resale.

#9 BICYCLES

Who hasn't owned a bike at least once in their life? I have sold bicycles since the start of my eBay career and I have never had one that I had a problem selling. All different types of bikes sell on the site; rather it is BMX, mountain, road or kid bikes.

My favorite place to purchase bicycles is on craigslist. Electronic bicycles are extremely popular and customers are willing to pay a premium for them. Vintage bicycles are also in high demand especially the Alex Moulton brand, which sell for over $4,000 each! Not only do vintage bikes sell, but also vintage frames can earn you instant cash. Schwinn frames sell for up to $300.

My best brands to sell: Apollo, Raleigh and Shimano.

#10 HIGH-END SUNGLASSES

Sunglasses are always an easy eBay sell and are a sellers dream. They are small, easy to ship, and profitable. Keep in mind that your glasses must be clean and in good physical shape in order to sell. Brands are the most important aspect of selling sunglasses. Profitable sunglass brands include: Oakley, Rayban, Louis Vuitton and Cartier. On a rare occasion, you can earn up to $1,500 per item if you sell the proper Rayban or Oakley glasses. These brands in particular are highly sought out by customers and more popular during the spring, and summer months.

Buying a "lot" of sunglasses can give you excellent profits consistently. You can also purchase these glasses bulk from reputable wholesalers.

#11 CURTAINS

You might be surprised that curtains are a hot selling item on eBay! If you have clean curtains that you never use anymore post them to eBay and watch how fast they sell. There tends to be lacks of supply for them, with a high demand so don't be afraid to post yours and make money. Curtains made out of silk and linen will sell the best. The two most popular brands are Pottery barn and Ethan Allen. Licensed curtains are also popular purchases such as Doctor Who, sports teams and Universities.

#12 VINTAGE BARBIE DOLLS

Barbie dolls are an American classic item and will forever be valuable. What little girl hasn't owned or played with a Barbie in her lifetime? Starting in 1959 the Barbie doll was modeled after the German doll named Bild Lilli. However, the company changed the doll's name, naming it after the creators (Ruth Handler) daughter.

Now with over a billion dolls sold in over 150 countries, Barbie's are the most popular doll in the world. With such the craze around the item, it is no wonder why vintage 1950's Barbie's in good shape can sell in the thousands. If you have an older version of the doll or a collectors Barbie doll you can easily sell it for hundreds of dollars on eBay. The Barbie has been changed several times, which is partially why the original model fetches such a hefty price tag. The most well-known change to the doll was the look of Barbie's eyes which changed in 1971. The changed caused the doll to look forward rather than the side eyed sexy look that occurred prior.

#13 LAPTOPS

Who doesn't need a laptop? Recent model laptops sell like hot cakes on eBay, considering, ever year laptops improve dramatically. Custom mod computers sell insanely well also. Top of the line computer modifications can sell close to $15,000.

Brands and requirements that sell the best: Gaming laptops, HP ENVY, Alienware, Razer Blade. These computers should include over 250 GB with recent processors. When selling laptops ensure that you place restrictions on buyers with bad payment history due to the fact that laptops tend to a high rate of buyers not paying.

#14 RIMS

As long as people drive cars, there will be a need for rims. Thankfully, for you, this makes a consistent market for anyone that sells them online or off. You might even be surprised how many people buy and sell rims on the site. Quite simply, rims are a goldmine on eBay, chrome rims in particular. I have bought rims for cheap on craigslist, at garage sales and even at junk yards and sold them on eBay with no problem. There are rims such as the Dub Spin 32" chrome that sell for over $10,000. However, specialty rims are not the only type that will sell. For example, four ford factory rim and 20" tire set recently sold for close to $1,500. Dodge challenger factory 20" wheels and rims sold for $1,500. Not bad right, with rims you never have to beg for a sell. Luxury car wheels and tires will sell for the highest price.

Best Brands: Ferrari, BMW, Audi, Porsche, Mercedes, Chevy truck rims, Gold Rims,

#15 TIRES

Just like rims, tires are a necessity for many people in the world. The typical rule is the larger the tires the more profitable it is to sell, given that they are in good condition with good amount thread on them. The best thing about selling tires is that they are not hard to find. Many of the tires I have sold just like rims I found on craigslist, mostly from people that were practically giving them away. Finding them is one aspect of success, but shipping is another. Tires are heavy and might be pricey to ship, it is good to account for this when buying them to resell.

#16 IPHONES

IPhone iPhones iPhones! These are well known sellers on the platform. I know sellers that literally make a living only selling iPhones on eBay. The great aspect of selling iPhones is that they sell for the market price rather than a discount price like most items on eBay.

The best iPhones to sell are iPhone 4's and up. Some iPhones can sell for insane amounts of cash. For example, IPhones that include the flappy bird application can sell for up to $25,000. Currently Apple iPhone 6's will sell for over $700. Even a broken iPhone 6 recently sold for over $200 and one with a cracked screen sold for $1,325. Keep in mind that an iPhone 4s with a cracked screen working can even sell for over $100, not bad huh.

I suggest getting a phone with clean ESN as bad ESN's dramatically lowers the price. A bad ESN means it cannot be activated with the carrier of the manufacturer. This could simply be because the original buyer had issues with the service or the phone was either lost or stolen. The problem is that most carriers won't reactivate a phone that has a bad ESN. With these phones, music, games apps and the internet are still accessible. You can check the esn on sites such as this swappa.com/esn and checkesnfree.com. You might also find unlocked phones which means the phone has been modified allowing it to be used by any carrier. Unlocked phones typically sell at a higher price. You can purchase them by searching for "iphone lots" on eBay, recycling companies, craigslist, offerup.com or Facebook buy and trade groups.

#17 IPADS

The Apple iPad is another hot item that everyone wants to have. IPad's are one of those items that someone will pay a premium price to obtain. The item isn't cheap, as the 4th Generation iPad sells for over $400. The IPad air 2 will sell for over $1,200 and will sell for over $150 even if broken. Even the iPad 1 broken will sell for $40. You can't go wrong with having an iPad in your possession. Just like iPhones you can buy them on sites such as craigslist, Facebook buy and sell groups, and offerup.com.

#18 IPODS

The Apple IPod is another huge seller and an item you can't go wrong with. Just like most apple items, the newest editions and collector's items sell the best. If you can find an iPod Nano 1st generation, you can sell it in any condition for close to $90. As Apple will buy it back for price if this item has returned due to a flaw with the item, which drives the cost up dramatically. I have found most of my iPods for sell on craigslist.

#19 MACBOOKS

MacBook's are pure gold on eBay. Unlike other PC computers, you can sell MacBook's years after the computer has been made as they are reliable, durable and consistent. I recently sold MacBook's from 2006 and 2007 for $300 each, not bad for a seven year old item. MacBook's even sell well broken, if you do this you want to make sure that you mention all the issues in the description. Customize MacBook's will sell for over $14,000 and new MacBook's can sell over $10,000.

#20 FLAT-SCREEN TELEVISIONS

Flat screen televisions are a staple in every department store and eBay isn't any different. If sell the proper brands you won't have any issues selling them. Keep in mind that televisions are fragile. Make sure that you bubble wrap and secure the item well while shipping. There are premium televisions that will sell extremely well, for example, a smart TV with Wi-Fi sell can sell for over $5000.

Televisions over 40" always sell well with the following Brands: Vzio, RCA, LG, Samsung, Sharp.

#21 ALL VIDEO GAME CONSOLES

Out of all the items I've sold on the site over the years, video games have remained the most consistent. The reason that they sell so well is that video games reach a huge global market with customers who love purchasing and collecting them. You will really hit the jackpot if you sell a rare item such as the Ultra-Vision Condor Attack for the Atari 2600 which recently sold for $45,000 or Super Copa for the Super Nintendo game that recently sold new for $6,900 or the Little Samson which recently sold for $5,1000 on Nintendo.

First person shooters sell the most and sports games sell the least. The PlayStation 2 console sells the least of all consoles, however, The Nintendo NES system sells extremely well. New consoles such as the PlayStation 4's and Xbox 360 are always top sellers and customers will buy them even if they are broken. Specialty video game add-on's such as the Sega Outback Trainer, NES duck hunt zapper and Rob the Robert controller are always a hit.

Consoles that sell: Nintendo, Nintendo 64, super Nintendo, Gameboy(all), virtual boy, PlayStation 1, PlayStation 3, PlayStation 4, PSP, Ps Vista, Atari

#22 HIGH-END FURNITURE

High End Furniture always sell well on the platform. Finding these items at garage sales is easier than you think. When buying and selling furniture it is important to ensure that, they are in excellent condition only. The best items to sell are dining room sets, sofa's, new king size bedroom sets, Handcrafted wood items, chairs and desks. Furniture can sell in the thousands on the site.

Brands to buy: Caspani, Versace, Herman Miller, Eames, Baker Furniture, Mahogany wood furniture.

#23 BOSE EQUIPMENT

You can't go wrong with Bose equipment. Every item they that offer is heavily purchased, even if they are old and broken. It is phenomenal that the company that started in 1964 is still popular to this day, selling over a billion dollars in products per year. Recently a new Bose lifestyle 535 entertainment system series sold for over $3,000 and Bose lifestyle v35 home theater used sold for $1,600. If you come across a Bose item of any kind, in any condition, buy it because there will be a demand for it.

Bose items: home speakers and subwoofers, headphones, audio player docks, home audio compact

#24 AUTHENTIC DESIGNER WATCHES

EBay is one of the biggest watch dealers in the world; although they don't advertise it as such their customers know this to be true. Designer watches are sold worldwide and are popular for various reasons on the site. If you didn't know how impactful they are, take a look on eBay yourself. Rolex watches can sell between $20,000 to $50,000. Watch prices vary dramatically based on the style and making of the watch. Brands such as such as Gucci can range from $150 to $3000. Watches are super cheap to ship and with proper bubble wrapping aren't very fragile. They are great items to sell through the bid process because the demand for them is so high.

Brands that sell: Armani Exchange, Cartier, Dolce & Gabbana ,Eddie Bauer, Emporio Armani, Gucci, Marc Jacobs, Michael Kors, Rolex, TAG Heuer, Tiffany & Co.

#25 SPECIALTY LEGOS

Who doesn't love Legos? The Lego group that was founded in 1932 and have been an American favorite ever since. The company produces over 5 million Lego bricks per hour and If you count the amount of Legos sold in a year, the amount would stretch across the world over 15 times. The company has been so consistent that a logo brick from the 1950's will still interlock with bricks being made today.

Legos are consistently good sellers, but even more popular are specialty logos such as star wars and star trek. These specialty Lego's are classic and rare, customers are willing to spend anything to acquire them. The most expensive Lego on the market is the Lego Star Wars Ultimate Collector's millennium falcon (10179) which currently sells for $3,800. Other pricy Legos are the Taj Maha 10189, which cost $3200 and the Grand Carousel that recently sold for $2500 (10196).

Specialty Legos that sell: DC Universe, Harry Potter, Ninjago, Avatar the last air bender, Xmen, Marvel, Mickey Mouse, Pirates of the Caribbean, Star Trek, Dora The Explorer, Halo and Barbie.

#26 GENERATORS

Who doesn't need a generator? They are electricity-producing devices that are used in power plants, in the home, motor vehicles, bikes, boats and more. This item has and will always be a popular sell on the website. Every different type, model, shape and size sells. Industrial generators tend to sell at the highest prices reaching as high as $20,000. However, you can sell single source generators for just as much.

 Even generator replacement parts and broken generators sell in the hundreds. You can find a generator to purchase on craigslist, newspaper classifieds and through companies such as dieselserviceandsupply.com/Used-Generators and machinerytrader.com.

It is good to know the exact status of any generator you buy. If you buy one used, assume you will need parts. I would advise that you have a technician look over it if you are selling it as working.

Good generator brands: John Deere, Onan, Detroit Diesel, Kohler, Caterpillar, and Cummings.

#27 DIAMONDS

Diamonds are a woman's best friend or a man's if you're selling them on eBay. I'm sure you know diamonds can be extremely valuable and nothing changes on eBay. The site is a hotbed for diamond buyers and sellers. Prices on any given day can reach up to $1,000,000. Yes, one million! I do advise that only experts that know what you are buying and selling trade in diamonds. If not you could possibly lose out big time. If you are an expert or are using one, just one transaction can prove to be life changing.

#28 HIGH-END APPLIANCES

Just like high-end furniture, high-end appliances sell. This is another item you can find on craigslist or in local classifieds. In many cases, you can purchase these items for very cheap. Keep in mind that profit is very important when buying and selling appliances, as it might be costly to ship, so making sure there will be leftover profits. It is not rare for high-end appliances to sell for over $5,000.

Appliances that sell well: Stainless steel, High Efficiently washer and dryers , double wall ovens, French door, Wine Cellar, Bottom Freezers and Cooktops

Brands that sell well: Wolf, Subzero refrigerator and freezer, Viking, Thermador, Gaggenau, Electrolux, Samsung.

#29 HIGH-END CLOTHING

Who doesn't love to wear the best of clothing? Well, those who buy on eBay do and it shows by their buying habits. Men's and women's brands alike sell extremely well along with All different types of clothing such as suits, jackets hoodies, jeans, skirt and dresses. I have had several high-end clothing items that literally have sold minutes after I post them to the site. Once you sell your first piece of clothing, it is easy to become addicted.

Brands that sell: Christian Dior, Dolce& Gabbana, Dooney & Bourke, Fendi, Giorgio Armani, Gucci, Hermes, Louis Vuitton, Neiman Marcus, Billionaire Boys Club, Ralph Lauren, Brioni, Tom Ford, Giannai Versace, Kiton, Yves Saint Laurent, Prada, Chanel, Burberry, Christian Dior, Moncler

#30 WALKMAN

Walkman's are one of my go to items to sell. This small and easily shippable item sells fast. I love to buy "lots" of these on the site and resell them individually. This method is the easiest money I've ever made on eBay to date. Walkman's are a high quality nostalgic item that we all know from our past and buyers love that. If you decide to sell Walkman's you can't go wrong. All varieties of Walkman's sell, this has been a hot item for years and the rarer they become the prices will continue to go up. If I don't buy Walkman's via eBay "lots" I will buy them at local vintage stores where I can typically find them for much cheaper than on eBay.

High priced Walkman's will make your bank account ring: The TPS-L2 Walkman, which was seen in the movie Guardians of the Galaxy currently sells for over $750 and the Sony Walkman WM 3 ex sells for $650. The Sony WM-D3 Walkman also sells for over $300. Walkman WM-WM800 sells for $250 and Sony Walkman WM-D6C over $200.

#31 DISCMAN

Like Walkman's, Discmans take people down memory lane and are still useful today. I have made good money selling Discman's, even some that haven't been in good shape either. Many Americans take what we have for granted and find it hard to believe that much of the world isn't caught up with our technology and still use devices such as the Discman normally. I purchase them the same way as Walkman's via eBay "lots", garage sales and vintage stores. From my experience, Discmans typically sell between $25-$35.

Rare and expensive Discmans: D-555 Discman sell for over $600 and the D-25 Sony sell for $150

#32 VOICE RECORDERS

I mentioned to one of my friends that works a 9 to 5 that one of the best sellers on eBay are my voice recorders. The complete shock and questioning on his face said it all. "Who buys them?" "What do they need them for?" "Can't they just use their cell phone?" My answer to all the questions was "I don't know, but they sell like it's nobody's business". This is very true, voice reorders especially Sony brand recorders; sell at all times a year, seven days a week, and three hundred sixty five days a year with ease. If you have them, post them to eBay and watch your money grow. I buy them in eBay "lots" consistently and even individually buying them low and selling them high. I have commonly come across Sony voice recorders that I purchase for $14 and sell for over $60. Selling voice recorders with batteries and tapes will add value to your recorder.

Voice Recorders best sellers: Olympus LS-100 $375, Olympus D-4000 $370, Sony Bm-575 $270

#33 QUALITY CASES FOR SMARTPHONE

Have a Otterbox, Urban Armor Gear or Lifeproof phone case? If you do, you will have no problem selling them. New phone cases always sell the best, but if your item is used and in good shape it still will demand value. These items sell well because they do exactly what they claim and that is protect your phone very well! The more recent the phone, the higher prices the case will be. I have placed these phone cases for one day bids at .99 (which I don't recommend) and have sold them for over $30, not bad for a one day eBay sale.

#34 WALKIE-TALKIES

Walkie-talkies are an everlasting item that are needed in many industries. Schools, fire departments, police forces, department stores and many more industries use them. Walkie-talkie buyers don't mind paying for what they need either.

Walkie-Talkie brands that sell: Motorola, Kenwood, cobra and Baofeng

#35 DIGITAL CAMERAS

One of the most common and easiest items to sell on eBay is digital cameras. Many people around the world don't have iPhones or superior gadgets, which make simple digital cameras perfect for their lifestyle. With a wide range of prices, there are also very high-end cameras that supersede anything you can get with a cell phone. Some of my favorite and easiest brands to get a hold of are Panasonic Lumix, Sony Cybershot and all Canon's.

#36 CAMCORDERS

Camcorders are similar to cameras and are a hot item to sell. The popularity of recording events is at an all-time high and so are camcorders. When selling them make sure your it works completely.

I have sold camcorders that I thought I tested only to find out that the items had issues.

Brands that sell: Sony, Canon, Panasonic, JVC, GoPro, Blackmagic

#37 TABLETS

Customers go crazy over Tablet devices. These versatile item is like a thin portable computer that can make your life astronomically easier. I have even sold broken tablets for good profit. The beauty of tablets is that they will sell in any condition; however, it is important to describe the current status.

Brands that sell: All brands, specifically Google nexus, Samsung Galaxy Note, Microsoft surface.

#38 EBOOK READERS

The eReader market is only growing with the emergence of more digital products and customers preferring eBooks over physical books. I know this firsthand, as I sold eReaders and couldn't keep enough in stock. This is another item that I sold while in broken conditions. Remember to still describe what is wrong with the eBook when selling broken. All working items sell for over $100.

Popular eBooks: Amazon Kindle, Barnes and Nobles Nook, Sony digital eBook

#39 SCIENTIFIC CALCULATORS

Scientific calculators are the perfect item to sell. I have never held on to a calculator longer than a week. They are small enough to ship for cheap yet have a huge demand. It is commonplace for them to sell for hundreds of dollars.

Top brands to sell: Hewett Packard, Casio, Texas Instrument

#40 TURNTABLES

Who doesn't like turntables? This item is in high demand and can carry a high price tag. I bought a turntable at a garage sale for $25 and later sold it for over $300, what a steal. The only concern you might have with turntables is shipping. You want to ensure that you wrap the item well as they can be a fragile ship.

Brands that sell well: Garrard, SME, TECHNICS, PIONEER, Yamaha, Kenwood, VIP Scout

#41 DRONES

If you are looking to sell an item for a large amount of money drones are the way to go. This can be octocopters or quadcopters; they all sell in the range of $50 to $4,800. If you so happen to get your hands on one, you don't have to worry about selling it even if it is broken. The love and passion for drones are uncanny to what I have seen in a niche market. Quite frankly, people love them and will buy them no matter the price.

#42 MILWAUKEE TOOLS

EBay is a great place to buy and sell tools. In this world of tools, it is hard to find a better selling product than the Milwaukee brand. Milwaukee offers everything from Drills to gardening tools. If you come across a Milwaukee brand item, buy it and sell it immediately!

43 DEWALT TOOLS

Similar to Milwaukee tools, Dewalt tools are beloved by customers. DeWalt mainly specializes in power tools that are top of the line. Many DeWalt Combo kits sell over $600 on eBay. Get ahold of a DeWalt item and post it to the site.

#44 SILK TIES

For customers eBay is one of the best places to buy ties due to the variety and prices the site offers in comparison to other tie suppliers. I typically sell my old ties, ties I purchased on eBay, and ties I buy at garage sales.

Ties brands loved by customers: Tom Ford, Hermes, Fendi, Louis Vuitton and Versace.

Characters ties such as The Simpsons, Mickey Mouse, Sports teams, Doctor Who, Harry Potter, College mascots, ford mustangs and Elvis Presley.

#45 HYDROPONICS

I recently started selling hydroponic items and I'm upset I didn't discover them sooner. It didn't take me long after my first few sales to realize that you can't go wrong selling hydroponics.

They sell for high margins and are extremely popular. I love hydroponics because they sell for over $50, which is rare for items on eBay. I'm warning you once you sell your first hydroponic item you might become hooked!

#46 MUSICAL INSTRUMENTS

Who hasn't tried an instrument at least once in their life? I still remember talking my parents into buying me my first set of drums in elementary school. As I remember, it cost close to $500. This still happens in households today, the only difference is there wasn't eBay back then. Now people of all ages buy their instruments online, with guitars being the most popular. Garage sales are a great place to buy these items.

Instruments that are popular buys: Microphones, keyboards, pianos, DJ mixers all should be in excellent condition to sell.

#47 GARAGE OPENERS

One hidden gem on eBay is the garage opener market. I was surprised stumbling upon this niche years ago when I won a storage auction that contained them and sold them all in three days. Ever since then I buy them whenever I can find them. Ensure you buy them in working condition and they practically sell themselves.

Brands that sell the best: Chamberlain, Craftsman, Liftmaster, Genie

#48 MARK LEVINSON EQUIPMENT

Mark Levinson sells various high-end audio equipment and has since the 1970's. Many Lexus car models feature Mark Levinson equipment because of its profound quality. Similar to Bose equipment all Mark Levinson items sell on eBay regardless of its status. Mark Levinson Amplifiers can sell for over $2,000. Even Mark Levinson adaptors will fetch for over $100.

Mark Levinson Equipment: Amplifiers, Pre-Amplifiers, Adaptors, power cords, power supplies, crossovers, tape machines.

#49 PREAMPLIFIER

Preamplifiers are another item that you can almost sell no matter what, even if broken. I loved finding preamplifiers at garage sells where sellers want to just get them out of their homes.

The profit on Preamplifiers are amazing and if you happen to find a high priced preamplifier such as a Marantz 7 you can sell them for over $15,000 price. Even though that is rare, preamplifiers are guaranteed to sell in the hundreds.

Popular brands: Adcom, Carver, Denon, McIntosh

#50 NUTRIBULLET

Nutribullet items are huge on eBay. Everything from the Nutribullet complete set to their replacement cups. Pick up one of these hot items and you won't hold on to them long. You can purchase them up at your local second hand store and sell for a respectable profit.

CONCLUSION

There it you have it: 50 items that you can always make money with on eBay. Hopefully, this information will help you on your eBay journey. Please keep in mind that other factors do come into play when buying and selling your items such as customer service, feedback, shipping time, and shipping charges. Always look at the completed listings on eBay to know what your product last sold for.

I also have a complete eBay guide that explains exactly how I earned a living selling items on eBay. This book is jam-packed with useful information that will undeniably help you. Sell on Ebay and Win: How to Build an eBay Empire With $100

Other Books by the Author:

Make Money Online: 70 Painless Way to Make Money for $5 or Less By Marc Pierce

Sell On EBay And Win: How to Start an eBay Empire with $100 By Marc Pierce

Increase Website Traffic Now: 45 Proven Tips Will Increase Your Website Traffic by 500% in the Next 45 Days By Marc Pierce

11825654R00028

Printed in Great Britain
by Amazon.co.uk, Ltd.,
Marston Gate.